the problem with having a body

the problem with having a body

jessica popeski

jessica popeski

GORDON HILL PRESS

Guelph, Ontario

Edited by Shane Neilson
Cover image by Alex Garant
Cover and book design by Jeremy Luke Hill
Proofread by Mary Hamilton
Set in Linux Libertine and Century Gothic
Printed on Mohawk Via Felt
Printed and bound by Arkay Design & Print

LIBRARY AND ARCHIVES CANADA CATALOGUING IN PUBLICATION

Title: The problem with having a body / Jessica Popeski.
Names: Popeski, Jessica, author.
Identifiers: Canadiana (print) 20250154889 | Canadiana (ebook) 20250157195 | ISBN 9781774221648 (softcover) | ISBN 9781774221655 (PDF) | ISBN 9781774221662 (EPUB)
Subjects: LCGFT: Poetry.
Classification: LCC PS8631.O6445 P76 2025 | DDC C811/.6—dc23

ONTARIO ARTS COUNCIL
CONSEIL DES ARTS DE L'ONTARIO
an Ontario government agency
un organisme du gouvernement de l'Ontario
Canada Council for the Arts
Conseil des arts du Canada
ONTARIO CREATES | ONTARIO CRÉATIF

Gordon Hill Press gratefully acknowledges the support of the Canada Council for the Arts, the Ontario Arts Council, and the Ontario Book Publishing Tax Credit.

Gordon Hill Press respectfully acknowledges the ancestral homelands of the Attawandaron, Anishinaabe, Haudenosaunee, and Métis Peoples, and recognizes that we are situated on Treaty 3 territory, the traditional territory of Mississaugas of the Credit First Nation.

Gordon Hill Press also recognizes and supports the diverse persons who make up its community, regardless of race, age, culture, ability, ethnicity, nationality, gender identity and expression, sexual orientation, marital status, religious affiliation, and socioeconomic status.

Gordon Hill Press
130 Dublin Street North
Guelph, Ontario, Canada
N1H 4N4
www.gordonhillpress.com

this is a fear one can have while lying in a hammock on a beautiful day.

— mary ruefle, *on fear*

table of contents

i. the pros and cons of staying sick

i. the pros and cons of staying sick

tuesday

pigeons upholster a wire. the sky diffuses, apricot to
coffee-ground black. i pick off nail polish like it's
my job, don't—quietly—don't, don't eat exactly sixteen

grapes (every night). amalgamate skittering thoughts;
midges in a net. *me step-grandad sold cigarettes from*
a dispenser on t kitchen wall, smoked most ov em

iz sen, lungz congested wi cancer, treacle-like tar.
i backspace a comma; consider a semicolon. below,
a streetcar bells. its tristan chord stacks an augmented

fourth, sixth, and ninth above the bass, elicits a wince,
like chewing lime when expecting tangerine, segments
riddled with pips, maggot-white. my maine coon,

spine turned, rearranges his coat on the arm of the settee.
cats don't worry about being seen as antisocial, walk
away when they've had enough human, will stalk a wiggle

of string, suspend disbelief, imagine a vole. my shoulders
are up to my earlobes, the stiffness of over-pumped tyres.
you visit, undisclosed. there's a better way to cook.

you are glassy. you are lavender in my pillowcase. later,
water stutters, kneads me. my voice will never be more
radiant than in the bathroom with the shower on full.

flatline

for jessica(s)

i

when it rains it drizzles ceaselessly
so everything gets soaked

in my dreams i sleep
            until six

ribs are scaffolding
stretch skin like cellophane
over leftovers

ii

grated inside out
by a gang
of moths
    their hooligan wings

she won’t make it through the night

iii

sudafed-drunk
a purposeful od
on call to hit
book flight
at the
            drop
            of a held hand

i text
            please keep me posted
                        twelve times
            had a muffin for breakfast
                              yeah right
autocorrect predicts words
that start with
c will be cat
            a for anxiety

binge on radio
            shurrup brain
writing worries on vulnerable pink

wet nurse futility
            loss

iv

remember her arm in pickle jar juice
up to her elbow
blue bottles belly-up
in the crimps of curtains

kalinka moya!
everyone needs their peck of dirt

v

a biro explodes its black bowels
in my backpack
bloodies everything

i find a ttc token
and a ten pound note
in the breast pocket of my autumn coat
                                        i am not stung by a bee

her paintings populate my walls
i inherited her cat
                    he throws himself at the window
                              at blue tits barking
                              in the nude arms of an ash

          the drill from condo construction
drones the unshakeable *f* of a
                    flatline

found

after georgia o'keeffe, linda pastan, richard siken, sylvia plath, raymond carver, & mikko harvey

i have done nothing all
summer but wait for

myself to be myself
again. the sun oozes;

cerulean sky; a clot
of swallows overhead.

i peel my own orange,
gorge every segment,

globes of juice darting
to my wrists & chin,

swaddle my pain in my
arms until it sleeps in

an unlit room. i haven't
shouted since the ground

snarled with ice, salt-teeth
stinging. how much can

i change before it turns
into murder? please, i'm

desperate to get what i
want, even so, for the

good things to happen,
for the asters to hurry,

for the lindens to blush,
for someone to forget

a glove in my life &
come back for it later.

this is how you lose me

bees are out
on the razzle:

pollen-drunk.
the triumph

of their butterfly
milkweed &

lavender habit.
grackles, in their

velveteen green,
tell tales over

how you erupt;
my mum would

have kittens
if she knew.

please soften
& not only when

you're on a
comedown.

this is how you
lose me. i won't

eat for days, &
dream of folding

myself through
the tissuey air

of the humber
bay arch bridge.

hospital is home

on the fourteenth floor, you know
you're in for the duration. not

the rapid-fire turnover of the twelfth,
booting patients on their third day,

ready or not, budget ballooning
(like your bowel) to bursting.

there's a community,
congregating on couches, here

beside the vending machine
bloated with treats we cannot eat,

iv pumps whining in discord
to be plugged in. we barter,

like farmer's market goers in saturday
morning sun, for sugar sachets

on meal trays of prune juice and broth,
swap snack-pack jellies for applesauce,

whatever the machinery of our middles
can mince. and i'm ashamed

of my anxiety—nearing four weeks
post-op, yo-yoing between hospital and home—

when i'm told *this is my month three,*
or five or eight. hospital is home,

surgery pending, limbs pencil-skinny,
belly shutting up shop.

blue

april. visit your gp because you can't shake this blue. it's darkening. navy nightshade. squid-ink indigo, borderline black. you can't scrub your skin with nailbrush bristles because it burrowed, like a tick. injected its innards. made your blood run blue. he asks you if you're sleeping, eating. no. he seems afraid of you. of your blueness and your womanness combined. he prescribes you trazodone, for sleep. refers you to mount sinai's psychiatric ward (the same hospital that will remove your colon the following march). await your appointment. ring your mother. how her voice tethers when you spiral, like a helium balloon released by a fist. may. revisit gp. still not sleeping, eating. coal-coloured clouds grow hands. wring your neck like a beer-wet bar rag, you say. *are you a threat to yourself or others?* by now, the blue has taken root. the blue of lips surrounding chattering teeth. the blue of rot. a decomposing blue.

two piece

shock of summer in may;
everyone's outside. rompers,
shades, saucer wide, double
denim, bellwoods brewery

ipas in bicycle baskets.
vintage at college &
ossington; dresses dangle
from rails: rayon, viscose,

crepe. short shorts in discount
bins: aqua stripes, mauve tulips.
what's inside is too much,
thrifted by pickers, retro sequined

to catwalk pomp and prices.
curbside baskets call *bargain!*
bikinis, migraine onset
fluorescent, decadent floral,

raring for cherry beach in
august, until i remember the
hot pink flesh zipper on my belly,
how it ruches and pleats the skin

that surrounds it, how,
like a clone, they took my belly
button with my colon,
how i'll never be able to cover it again.

now we are twenty-six

our neighbours are tea drinkers.
the kettle singing at seven-thirty

is all we hear across the hall. i sleep
one way, corpse-flat, left shoulder

shoved under a mashed pillow,
face tilted to blanks between the

blinds. re-reading, i find numbers
penciled in books, calories counted.

in the shower, like goldilocks,
a stickler, the water a touch cold or

hot, never just right. the salve of
fresh sheets, makeup removed.

nails lacquered, accentuating the line
of the moon, i am a girl who, for a

ringing phone or a tall can cracked on
a patio below, drops exactly nothing.

i attempt from luv's sickness

after henry purcell

: i attempt from luv's sickness
to fly in vain
since i am myself my own fevuh
since i am myself my own fevuh
and pain :

no more now
no more now
fond heart
wi pride no more swell
thou canst noh raiz forsuz
thou canst noh raiz forsuz
enuf to rebel

: i attempt from luv's sickness
to fly in vain
since i am myself my own fevuh
since i am myself my own fevuh
and pain :

for luv haz more power
an less mercy than fate
to make uz seek ruin
to make uz seek ruin
an luv thoze that hate

: i attempt from luv's sickness
to fly in vain
since i am myself my own fevuh
since i am myself my own fevuh
and pain :

stunner

a stunner of a day for pro-lifers on the
northeast corner of logan & gerrard.
i'm sixteen, suddenly. a globule of cells

shreds my fallopian tube; i collapse to
my iv alarm's dissonance; blood swamps
my shoulders; i beg for them to be

crowbarred free. a hell of a summer;
sun scorches the tips of cedar & ash;
waxwings in rowdy flight; hydrangeas,

dusty, gasp among chants & foul graphics,
faux fetuses glommed in ketchup & paint;
placarded men chorus like it's their job

to remind me how two abortions at thirty-
one saved me from a future of smashed glass
& cheekbones, of chairs splintered in half.

because

or why you keep on doing it; after di brandt

why you keep on doing it, getting up out of bed, the jumbled sheets, the sun a salve, storm ripening in your skull, night tart in your mouth, walking barefooted to the kitchen to fill the kettle, snap on the stove, its *clack clack clack*, pour coffee granules into a cup, dust crumbs from the counter, move into the routineless morning.

because your nephew crams your screen, gap-toothy, rosy, & rotund, tries to stand, legs spindly like a lamb's.

because the branches of the ash through the window, up the stairs, blossoming the porch, cheer the sky along.

because your students, like you, far from family, appear in your inbox, offering good health, the promise of face masks to spare.

because there are phone calls, in abundance, just because.

because there are virtual orchestrations of berlioz, mendelssohn, brahms, one-woman choirs, yoga, unisoned breath, streaming.

because the earth, ignoring her ailments, is there, every morning, gorgeous, grand beneath your feet, carouselling the cosmos, keeping you safe, not stuck, at home.

because the moon, sickled, incandescent, stays, endures, even in crisis, unafraid, nightlighting this gloom.

a whole damn moon

can we chronicle the sky?
cornflower with milk white
apostrophe stars strung in its

abundance. a neighbour at my
door knocking, one hand a
fistful of daffodils, their canary

trumpets, the other catching
& cooing over my heart as it
runs amok. i want to be

swaddled like that, the ghost
of tissue paper hugging stems,
fingers permed around ribbon.

compose me an incantation
for splendour, a poesy for the
medicine of honeyed tea, another

for the ritual of sudsing & soaking
our rottweiler's dish. he makes it
look easy: his boundless joy, barks

ricocheting the graffitied underpass;
yes, you are prairifire blossom;
yes, you are a whole damn moon.

last child in the woods

after richard louv

i

rain-bashed yard,
yarrow skirts fraying.

branch fingers scissor
cardinal-yellow light.

cicadas brawl.
magpie, warbler, thrush.

tiptoed, hands starfished,
breath fogging

french windows.
a pair of plum-red

smacked bottoms for
grubbying the glass.

ii

mother-in-law's tongue
on the counter, reeking

lysol. yellow-green
rug moss between toes.

wall, cerulean sky.
cosmos confined to a

computer screen square.
blue-headed vireos

belong in books, and
ruby-crowned kinglets,

white-breasted nuthatches.
aurora borealis clotting

over prairie suburb sprawl
will be watched on television.

iii

a tomcat carries
mouthfuls of mouse
across the lawn.

her room is glitter.
sparkle shards
snowflaked to the carpet.

on each foot a different
shoe, one that shotguns stars
when she stomps.

plastic constellations.
she practices port de bras,
jeté, arabesque.

doorknob reimagined
as a barre.
a tutu cinches her

grapefruit belly.
the bulb button where
mommy says the

midwife didn't finish
her off right. through the
window, soil gunges

in flower beds.
peonies drool
remnants of rain.

there are mud pies
to be made, elbows and
knees to be muckied.

little girls belong inside.
skull stuffed
with such feathers.

erase

so much for a red-hot breton summer
the sky brews black; the peril of rain
chickens cuckoo on the doorstep

hydrangeas—brittany's adopted
flower—opulent in lavender
aquamarine, mother-die white pearl

our neighbour pulls up to the curb
hunched, smile hearty, holding
a bushel of broccoli like a bouquet

courgette like a police baton under
his armpit; potatoes bloodied in mud
quels gros légumes! i try *j'adore les légumes*

merci! my tongue in stirrups thinks in
german not french; *danke schön* familiar
a man with no fixed abode i jigsaw-puzzle

together *slit another man's throat in*
vannes for urinating against the wall of a
church after dredging a barrel of wine

his *vin rouge* marinates on the table
in a glass. *j'ai soixante-quinze ans*
j'ai vingt-sept ans i manage back: half his age

broaching *trente. la vie est courte*
he adds; another lifetime worth of
work, i think, to erase myself in full

persimmon season

grieve the end of persimmon season—
a year without their caramel flesh.

january unspools unendingly, sparrows
ballistic among the fractured elbows

of meadowsweet; the sky melts charcoal
to apricot, snow silver & curdling.

how can a body withstand this?
tape-measuring time by surgeries:

colon resections, an ectopic pregnancy,
an abortion, a crushed foot. your heart

smashes. every good shell you
hold—their velvet bellies, iridescent

lavender & pearl—splinters to shrapnel
in your hands. cling to your pitbull-poodle,

scrub your knuckles red, wash & rewash
her dish, your body protesting *no, no.*

turned around here

so much green you want to drink
it, roll in it, tail wagging, drunk as a dog.

in the grey pond fish
surface from the murky
beneath. their bull's-eye ripples.

the slide, rollercoaster-wild,
is no taller than you. the verge
you log roll is grassy, aflame,

daffodil starry. you get so
turned around here. fold your
feelings into frightened squares,

muddle them in the belly of a hat.
remove them, smooth

them, align them, one by one.

falling

& then, another dream of falling, forever
falling, past incisor stars, down the throat
of the abyss. dream of your bicycle chain,

rusted red, & fingernails, falling, clean off.
of your sewing machine catching, snaffling,
coughing thread. of your sister remarrying,

& you've lost your speech, your gown,
eyelids mascara-spattered. of sea creatures,
razor-toothed, gills bloating, urchins

beckoning; you've snagged your calf on
coral, blood ballooning, forgotten how
to front crawl. dream of your grandmother

as your grandmother, as a kitten, silken,
slinking figure eights around your ankles,
as a baby, frilled, dusk-cheeked, disks of veg

bubbling on the stove, impossible desserts
crowding the table, glittered jellies, steamed
puddings, immaculate madeleines you gorge.

the wrong place

a nearly full moon,
chalk disk on black
and lilac smudged
sky; alone. stars
snuffed out in cloud

pockets. wind elbows
thorn-crowned
thistles, skinny weeds
romping. i watch
from the window

a crank in the bowl
of my belly, its fog
carouselling. sharper
now, severing meat.
a circular mammal

slinks to the pit
of my shoulders,
gorging bone
branches. *i wish*
i would die, i say.

let it be wings laddering
flesh into feathers
to fly me. cardinal
riverbanks burst,
cranberry clots on cotton,

reservoir of blood.
everything silver,
bleached clean.
little fiddlehead unfurling,
you can't grow there.

exile

don't you want to be alive before you die? — anthony doerr

a prayer can be anything:
this lilac morning, its navy
blue branches, & sparrow
specs. i slice a radish &
think of you; everyone has
the right to disappear. on

our walks, the streets teem
with blossom: butter &
peach-pearl. here's something
i wonder: because my puppy
was born in winter, was young
in winter, does she know

instinctively there is a summer
to come, or will it be a surprise?
i have a throat full of russian;
not nonsense: nursery rhymes.
i reread my sent emails to
remind me who i am, slather

cream on the reptilian skin
of my knuckles and wrists,
crosshatched by papercuts;
everyone has the right to do away
with themselves if they want.
pain zigzags; i exile my foot to

forget when it was ripped off,
flesh-seams fraying, dangling
by a ribbon of ligament,
selvage scrapped. i'm ragweed-
skinny, again. remember: now
all the nice things mean nothing.

aren't you worried?

aren't you worried
that the ghost of an

onion lurks at your
fingertips? that garlic

peppers your mouth?
that dish soap bubbles,

radioactive cyan, web
your toes? that a strand

of hair sticks to the
toxicity of lip gloss?

that spores erupt on
your dogs' muzzles

from chicken bones
spat onto the street?

that foam will form
on their dishes? that

avocados fur & fall
at their feet? that the

grass you run through
is maggoted with

bacteria & carpets
your hardwood floors?

come clean

vexation, and torment. says that her mind forces her always to think of eating. feels herself degraded by this. has entirely, for the first time in years, stopped writing poetry. — frank bidart

i

a sparrow clatters
to the patio

grubbied by the city
he remains white-cheeked
black-bibbed
wings hickory brown
lap-cat tame

he inspects the cashew
centrepiece the hostess left
despite my

no
please
no food
menus a heaped monument

revolted by friends who
arriving late
forgot to eat first

ii

superbly hot
sun bouncy-balls the sidewalk

a pug puffs audibly
on a lead

cyclists dismount
under a drumming
canopy of bees
rosemary and pin oak
drunk

children dingle in one and
two pieces from
monkey bars
awaiting the eternity of an
hour after eating
to swim

in a frozen yogurt spot
i try to
come clean

palms belly-up
beta-carotene yellow
but think better
of my order

return to the road
its applauding heat
to *ma'am! miss!*

my proposed cup
its contents
on the counter
congealing

iii

i slit my skin
when shaving
my legs
mouths of blood
that won't shut up

absurdly early
on the subway platform
watching the train headlights
torch the tunnel
i unstick a plaster
it's been three days, i think
it's over

it jewels my ankle
bolts like lava
reddening my sock
i wonder
what mineral i'm missing

iv

markham's interlocking leaves
that tweenage hand trick
here's the church here's the steeple
a sugar, norway, silver, emerald queen maple
and tulip, redmond linden, hackberry, horse chestnut
schubert chokecherry marquee

a willow drizzles to tarmac at harbord
the pong of a skunk feast
a block below bloor
candy cane spatter
meat fly-amassed

not supposed to bike but i bike
the way my body overburns

around ramhorn handles
nails tipped maroon shellac
all my rings are falling off my fingers

v

up always at six at the latest
apply hides of mascara
get out immediately

on the lawn surrounding the pool
a chorus of daisies
i allow myself a peach
let it dribble
from forearm to elbow

the cymbal-splash of swimmers
the trill of a starling in flight
clouds dilate northwest
sunbathers splay limbs like professionals
slant books to avoid tan lines
as if it was a sport

a woman i often see in the elevator
with veined kale sprouting from her corduroy tote
aligns herself in an arrow
dives deep and resurfaces
steadies herself on overlapping arms

in conversation at the lip of the pool
hair lacquered to her head
she wishes she was shorter
itemizes her female friends of preferable heights

and despite an irritating
uninterrupted discussion
about party cups
sun-warm cider and the procurement of ice
i stay
to prolong the time between waking and eating

vi

my wine glass weeps
long legs slipping
swollen sides

only women
work here

glittered
leggy
modelesque
the cosmos of them
twinkling

dress hems severed
bottom-cheek short

i sausage-roll my scarf
onto the seat
a barrier stopping its
wooded slats from
digging in

the two-pronged pain
of my ilium pushing
through flesh

from behind
vertebrae knots
easily counted
above a backless dress

vii

old friend
from out-of-town
asks to meet two hours
beyond my bedtime
it's been years

since i wore the weight of another woman
distributed evenly across my body

we drink
various wince-worthy somethings
on rocks
he's surprised
the street seems quiet for the city
stucco-starred sky
a handsome moon
cross-stitched by pine
its knitting-needle leaves

he pulls up a picture of his girlfriend
assures *this is her*
at her biggest
i wonder if he saves this
shoptalk
for me

viii

at a party
in the bee-yellow jumper i sleep in
because dolling up is an ordeal
—lied to, *looks lovely*
waffle-knit boxy over bones

i shoot vodka with ibuprofen
the sugar-coated cranberry-looking kind

the oven hiccups
spring rolls onto a tray
grease-encrusted stalagmites
lime eighths film over on the counter
a caucus of blundstones by the door

i discuss my maine coon's imperatives
with another cat mum
his bizarrely tempting
human-grade chicken au jus
sulk on my coat before i
turn into a pumpkin at twelve

what's a reasonable time frame to be social?
i ask my uber driver
honest ed's bulbs blur
through just-washed windows
palmerston coyly lamp-lit
the frump-frump of speed bumps
reminding my ribs
i over-downward-dogged
is half an hour enough?

ix

the waitress grants
me immediate friendship

our accents
synthesized as other
by eavesdroppers
although to us
nothing alike

the honey locust listens
snaps its
lozenge leaves

she's irish
from cork
the auditorium of its harbour
whose sacred spaces
i sang in at their
international choral festival
during my teens
triskel christchurch
masonic hall
cathedral of st. mary
and st. anne

how our milky ways align
this her moonlight

by day
a receptionist at the
dance studio where i took
ballet, broadway, barre
before getting sick i say
scar tissue handcuffing
my esophagus
pulling taut

the real reason:
ashamed of seeing
my string limbs
in wall-to-wall
floor-to-ceiling mirrors

x

in the too-cool clinic
furnished in sealskin velveteen
cleverly mirrorless—
price-tagged privatization

my dietician asks for a list
the pros and cons of staying sick
marquise and asscher diamantés
tinkle from a lampshade
the strained exhalation of her computer on her desk
for next time

outside
queued boutiques of astounding specificity
epicurean dog treats
a millinery
ladies' tunics in varying weights of linen

i sulk southbound
an irish setter holds her lead between her teeth
takes her human for a walk
bumbles over rotund paws
a bone bells from her red collar

i chip the thumb of my
wedgewood-blue manicure
panic
get it patched in the nearest salon
perfect again

in the black glass of an unopened bar
stools overturned on tables
the deep vs of my cheeks
sun-rosed shoulders and knees
muscles loose and stringy

i set up in a semicircular park
grass fanning from its bandstand
clover zigzagging their purple heads
shake my scarf into a blanket
pinch my belt into my belly
on a fresh page
underline *pros*

xi

i am the skeleton
in the corner
an exhibition of bones
nursing the gunged leftovers of a cold
sniffing non-stop
how i always sneeze twice

i arrived as the creperie opened
to *observe normalized eating*
watched the sky drain
milk to peony to cornflower blue
stars snuffed
cherry blossom buds
loosening their fists

books stud the table
stamp-square
pages leafed
corners curling

my pencil fingers
peel an orange–
the satisfaction
of ripping pithy core
from flesh

the noisy business of breakfast
a little girl with a
centre part and plaits
dissects a pancake
oragamied into a triangle
rocket leaves licked with oil
a croissant
pillowy
overstuffed with almond
zig-zagged with chocolate
while her mother
swats flakes from the bib of her dress

xii

open beating your eating disorder:
a cognitive-behavioural self-help
guide for adult sufferers to page xi.

a smashed weetabix & teaspoon
of zero percent yogurt slimes
over under cling film in the fridge;

av yu ad yer breakfast?
bio bifidus regularis spores erupt
into ecosystems of their own.

twelve oranges elbow each other
in a scab-red bowl on the sill;
reflect miniature sun-specks.

a red-billed chough chortles from
a bay leaf laurel; the cirrus sky
coughs, holiday-postcard blue.

no green woodpecker has broadcasted
itself yet—its meditative *tap tap tap.*
lavender is rampant; bees romp.

fires in the luberon the bbc announces
have killed off ninety-eight percent
of the area's wildlife; repopulation

could take four to five years; i catch
my ragged spine in the mirror,
brittle bird-boned body, google symptoms

of heart failure, kidney failure,
liver disease, & how many calories
per slice of brown bread.

xiii

there are women in the story of a support group
they meet beneath lancet windows
unbiased white walls
dome ceilings
the flush of antiseptic light
silver belly of a tern as it passes
water in a jug on a table in the corner
marinating disks of lemon

their age gaps are generous
generations
they look nothing and everything alike
at the extremes of their bodies

they talk and talk
it smarts
ghosts trolling
pasts niggling
phobias manifesting physically
germs, food, slitting, drugs, obsessive compulsion
entirely different but somehow the same

and one woman
older
behind bifocals
hair feathered
gnatcatcher-grey
talks of time
the terror of it
eaten alive
if only she had more time

the room in its semicircle
sits up
a ruler-straight row
the youngest faces rose-redden
knowing this is what they have

all the things that come with a person leaving

move as if through honey: slower than you'd
like, to grow stronger than you are. remember
this: if your head's a spinning top at bedtime,
it's enough just to close your eyes & rest. gauge

the bird by its song: the surprise of an owl's
hoo hoo hoo at lunchtime, arrow geese overhead.
pansies suckle the windowsill; an oratorio from
eggshells shattered in the sink. the almond,

flowering, is another way of harnessing hope;
the buttercup cheers you, yellows your chin;
clouds crochet away the burgeoning stars. i want
to tell you all the things that come with a person

leaving, the abundance of jumpers, of cotton
lawn, the single piece of silver you box & sharpie
keep. unfold & refold your grief, shake it out,
make it small, & get on with it. keep your new

shoes off the table; never sew with pins lining
your lips, & when the oranges are round & ripe,
eat, let juice trickle becks to your elbows, litter the
garden with their peel & pith, keep the slugs away.

the problem with having a body

at least it's this time today;
velveteen sunrise, up with
the swifts, their gossip.

the problem with having a
body is you have to carry

it everywhere with you.
mine has held the curlicue
of three babies & still

i've no one to show for it;
a hoard of manila medical

files cramped & yellowing.
at night i constellate stars
into dreamsongs for two

working feet, sleepskate
the lake, iron out the facia

of my butchered belly, wake
to a great dane in the dog
park straining to hear her

human, a house finch, crimson-
faced, fussing, earwigging

cranes, & sink into the same
morningly loss, the verity of
my bones, spattered on the bed.

ii. sculptured

ii. sculptured

university health network

naproxen remeron
sertraline clonazepam
trazodone quetiapine
zopiclone pantoprazole
zofran docusate
sodium polyethylene
risperidone cipralex
gravol imigran
morphine lyrica
dilaudid celebrex

naproxen remeron
sertraline clonazepam
trazodone quetiapine
zopiclone pantoprazole
zofran docusate
sodium polyethylene
risperidone cipralex
gravol imigran
morphine lyrica
dilaudid celebrex

naproxen remeron
sertraline clonazepam
trazodone quetiapine
zopiclone pantoprazole
zofran docusate
sodium polyethylene
risperidone cipralex
gravol imigran
morphine lyrica
dilaudid celebrex

naproxen remeron
sertraline clonazepam
trazodone quetiapine
zopiclone pantoprazole
zofran docusate
sodium polyethylene
risperidone cipralex
gravol imigran
morphine lyrica
dilaudid celebrex

naproxen remeron
sertraline clonazepam
trazodone quetiapine
zopiclone pantoprazole
zofran docusate
sodium polyethylene
risperidone cipralex
gravol imigran
morphine lyrica
dilaudid celebrex

healthy

#foodporn #run
#foodporn #run #love
#foodporn #run #love
            #foodporn #run #love
            #foodporn #run #love
            #foodporn #run #love
                        #foodporn #run #love
                        #foodporn #run #love
                        #foodporn #run #love #fresh
                                    #foodporn #run #love
                                    #foodporn #run #love #fresh
                                    #foodporn #run #love #fresh
                                                #foodporn #run #love #fresh
                                                #foodporn #run #love #fresh
                                                #foodporn #run #love #fresh

underweight

#yum
#yum
#yum
#yum #healthy
#yum #healthy
#yum #healthy
#yum #healthy #eatclean
#yum #healthy #eatclean
#yum #healthy #eatclean
#yum #healthy #eatclean #foodgasm
#yum #healthy #eatclean #foodgasm
#yum #healthy #eatclean #foodgasm
#yum #healthy #eatclean #foodgasm #likemypic
#yum #healthy #eatclean #foodgasm #likemypic
#yum #healthy #eatclean #foodgasm #likemypic #passion
#yum #healthy #eatclean #foodgasm #likemypic #passion
#yum #healthy #eatclean #foodgasm #likemypic #passion
#yum #healthy #eatclean #foodgasm #likemypic #passion #diet
#yum #healthy #eatclean #foodgasm #likemypic #passion #diet
#yum #healthy #eatclean #foodgasm #likemypic #passion #diet

overweight

#fitfood #madewithlove #eat
#fitfood #madewithlove
#fitfood #madewithlove #eat
#fitfood #madewithlove
#fitfood #madewithlove #eat
#fitfood #madewithlove #eat
#fitfood #madewithlove #eat
#fitfood #madewithlove #eat
#fitfood #madewithlove #eat
#fitfood #madewithlove #eat

obese

#pigout #sweettooth #foodcoma #cake
#pigout #sweettooth #foodcoma #cake #cook
            #sweettooth #foodcoma #cake #cook
            #sweettooth #foodcoma #cake #cook #fattofit
                        #sweettooth #foodcoma #cake #cook #fattofit
                        #sweettooth #foodcoma #cake #cook #fattofit

extremely obese

#weights #healthy #carbs #skinny #paleo #fit #discipline #dinner
#healthy #carbs #skinny #paleo #fit #discipline #dinner
#healthy #carbs #skinny #paleo #fit #discipline #dinner
#carbs #skinny #paleo #fit #discipline #dinner
#skinny #paleo #fit #discipline #dinner
#skinny #paleo #fit #discipline #dinner
#paleo #fit #discipline #dinner
#fit #discipline #dinner
#fit #discipline #dinner
#discipline #dinner
#dinner

muscle tension dysphonia false cords

after lindsay lalla

poco fa
heidenröslein
come unto him in the country
gekommen bright is the ring of words mädchen

fern hill mon cœur
s'ouvre à ta voix oft denk'
ich, sie sind nur alone, and yet alive
aus ausgegangen ave maria there is
der welt abhanden beauty in the bellow
voi, che sapete blast una voce
una donna a quindici anni
i have dreamed chacun a son goût
l'eau when i am laid in earth
das senza euridice les chemins de
may abide the day that labour love
his coming ständchen wind blows once
all ye you lose your heart babbino caro
d'amore fairest isle a weekend o mio

l'amour but who a green cornfield en sourdine blows as
che faro mondnacht au bord de
o bei nidi der tot und
die nacht

krrrrrr

krrrrrr
krrrrrr krrrrrr
krrrrrr krrrrrr krrrrrr
krrrrrr krrrrrr
krrrrrr
kreeee
kreeee kreeee
kreeee kreeee kreeee
kreeee kreeee
kreeee
kreeay
kreeay kreeay
kreeay kreeay kreeay
kreeay kreeay
kreeay
kraaay
kraaay kraaay
kraaay kraaay kraaay
kraaay kraaay
kraaay
kroooh
kroooh kroooh
kroooh kroooh kroooh
kroooh kroooh
kroooh

my oh my

ma ee oh
ma ee oh   ma ee oh
ma ee oh   ma

ma ee oh   my oh
ma ee oh   ma ee oh   my oh my oh
ma ee oh   ma   my oh   my

ma ee oh   my oh
ma ee oh   ma ee oh   my oh my oh
ma ee oh   ma   my oh   my

ma ee oh   my oh
ma ee oh   ma ee oh   my oh my oh
ma ee oh   ma   my oh   my

nyay

nyay
nyay ay ay nyay
nyay ay ay ay ay ay ay nyay
ay ay ay ay nyay ay ay ay ay ay
ay ay nyay ay nyay ay ay ay
nyay ay nyay ay

kay

kay
  kay   kay
     kay   kay   kay
         kay   kay   kay   kay
           kay   kay   kay   kay   kay
                        kay   kay   kay   kay
                                     kay   kay   kay
                                                 kay   kay
                                                              kay

no

no
no no
no no no
no no no no
noooooo no no no
noooooo no no
noooooo no
noooooo

notes & acknowledgements

Thank you to the generosity of the Ontario Graduate Scholarship committee, and to the board of the University of Guelph College of Arts Graduate Travel, Research, and Creation Fund for providing me with opportunities to conduct research for this project.

To Kevin Connolly, for reminding me to keep my stick on the ice, and Margaret Christakos, for voicing my fascination for the matrilineality of song. To Roo Borson, for encouraging my affinity for birds and trees, and to Di Brandt, for teaching me everything I know about ecofeminist poetics.

To Anstruther Press editor-in-chief, Jim Johnstone, whose careful edits to *The Wrong Place* live on in this collection. To my cohort and teachers in the University of Guelph's MFA program, where the seedling of this book took root.

To Shane Neilson and Jeremy Luke Hill of Gordon Hill Press for championing my work.

Immeasurable thanks to my Mummy, my sister, my Grannie, and my Maggie.

I am grateful to have written many of these poems while in Tkaronto, which is covered by Treaty 13 and the Williams Treaties, the traditional territories of the Mississaugas of the Credit, the Anishnabeg, the Chippewa, the Haudenosaunee, and the Wendat peoples.

Some poems in this collection have been featured in the following magazines, journals, and chapbook publications: Anstruther Press, *Reverie Literary Magazine, White Wall Review, Write Where We Are Now, League of Canadian Poets: Poetry Pause, The Woven Tale Press, Riddle Fence, Dusie, Hart House Review, carte blanche, swamp pink, Grain, Harbor Review*, and elsewhere.

"last child in the woods" is in dialogue with Richard Louv's book of the same title.

The final stanza of "now we are twenty-six" sparked from a line in J. D. Salinger's *Nine Stories: A Perfect Day for Bananafish.*

Frank Bidart's "Ellen West" granted me permission to write the sequence "come clean".

"all the things that come with a person leaving" took flight after reading Gillian Sze's "Instructions."

"because" borrows images from Di Brandt's "blue light, falling around us" from *Jerusalem, beloved.*

"muscle tension dysphonia" comprises exercises devised by soprano, singing teacher, and songwriter, Lindsay Lalla. Without her, I might have never sung again.

I have read, overheard, remembered, misremembered, and borrowed lines written by Naoise Dolan, Georgia O'Keeffe, Linda Pastan, Ellen Bass, Richard Siken, Sylvia Plath, Raymond Carver, Mikko Harvey, Jessica Johns, Kyla Jamieson, Henry Purcell, Mary Ruefle, Anthony Doerr, Helen Humphreys, and others.

biographical note

Jessica Popeski is a dis/abled opera singer, Professor of English, Creative Writing, and Music, and internationally published, intersectional ecofeminist poet. Her work has been published in *carte blanche, Leaf Press, Room, Hart House Review, Riddle Fence, The Woven Tale Press, Grain, Harbor Review, White Wall Review,* and elsewhere. She is the recipient of multiple scholarships and awards, was named one of Tkaronto's "exceptional up and coming writers" by Open Book, and authored *Oratorio* and *The Wrong Place* with Anstruther Press. She was raised, for the most part, in Moscow, Russia, and Sheffield, England, by her mother and grandmother, and is a Professor at Seneca Polytechnic, Humber Polytechnic, and George Brown College.